TODDLER

THANKSGIVING
COLORING BOOK

Holiday Coloring and Activity Book
for Toddlers and Preschoolers

PRESCHOOL ACTIVITY WORKBOOKS

ISBN-13: 978-1979457989 ISBN-10: 1979457980

THE *TODDLER THANKSGIVING COLORING BOOK* IS PERFECT FOR KEEPING YOUR TODDLER OR PRESCHOOL AGE CHILD ENTERTAINED AND BUSY THIS THANKSGIVING HOLIDAY SEASON WHILE ALSO HELPING THEM TO DEVELOP THE FINE MOTOR CONTROL THEY NEED FOR THE FUTURE AS THEY COLOR THESE FUN SIMPLE COLORING PAGES.

WHAT'S INSIDE:

- LARGE 8 X 10 INCH PAGES

- 30 FUN PICTURES TO COLOR

- 30 DUPLICATE COLORING PAGES YOU CAN COLOR WITH YOUR CHILD OR THEY CAN SHARE WITH A FRIEND

What are you THANKFUL For?

Draw your favorite food on the plate

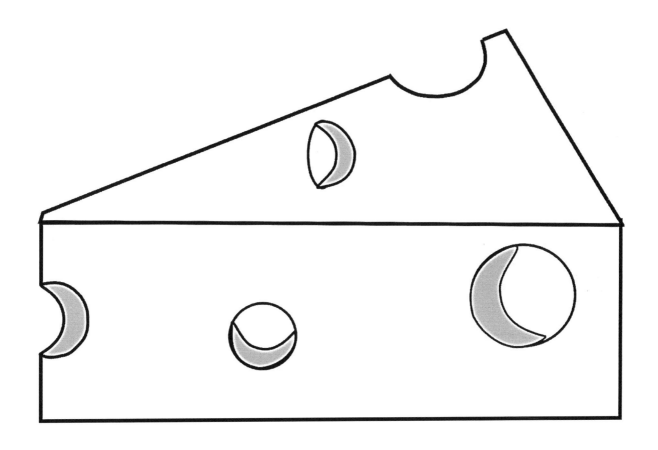

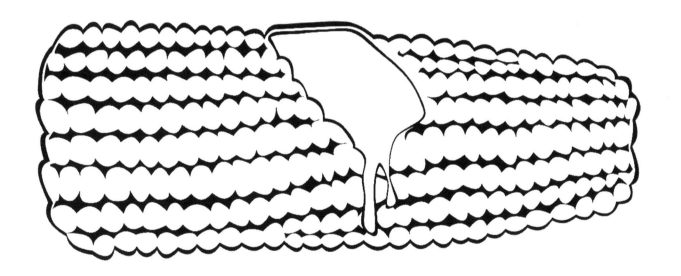

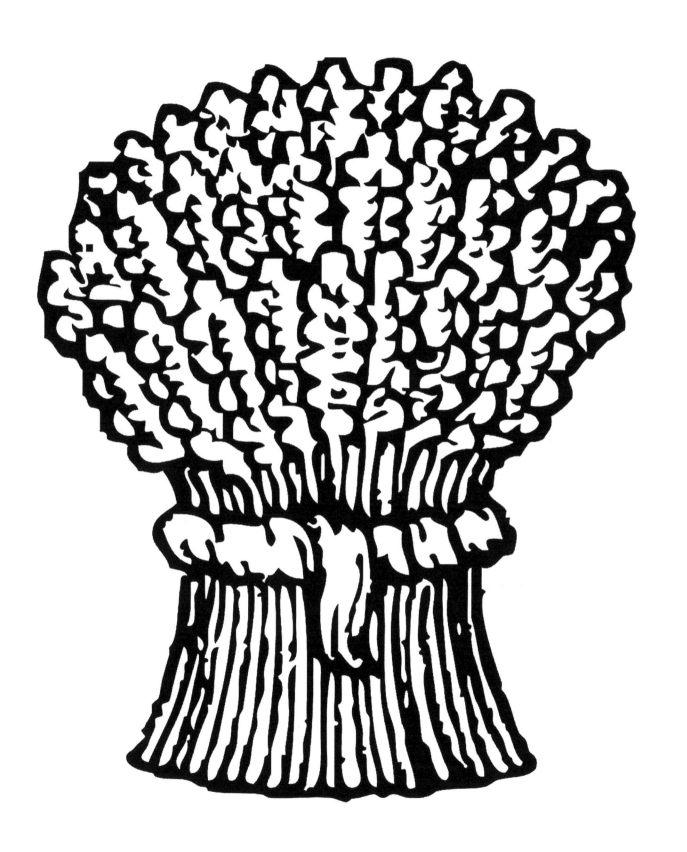

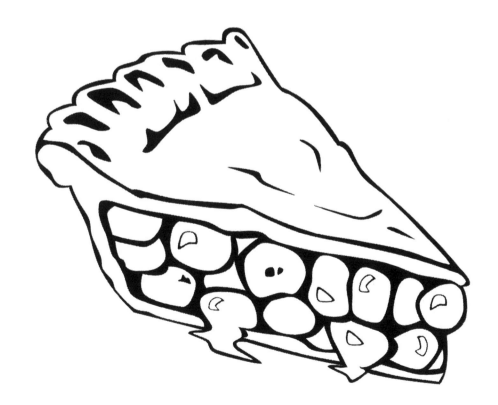

Share a coloring page with a friend

What are you THANKFUL For?

Draw your favorite food on the plate

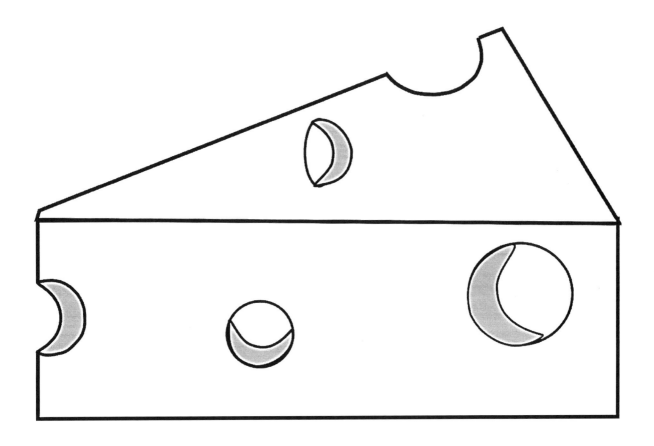

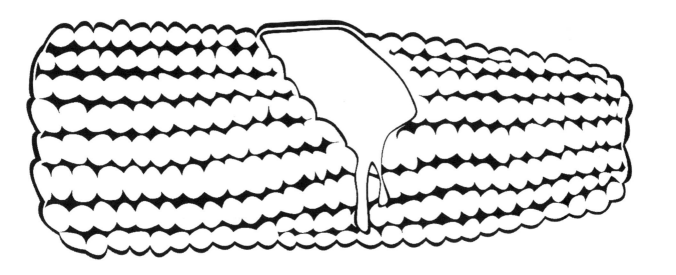

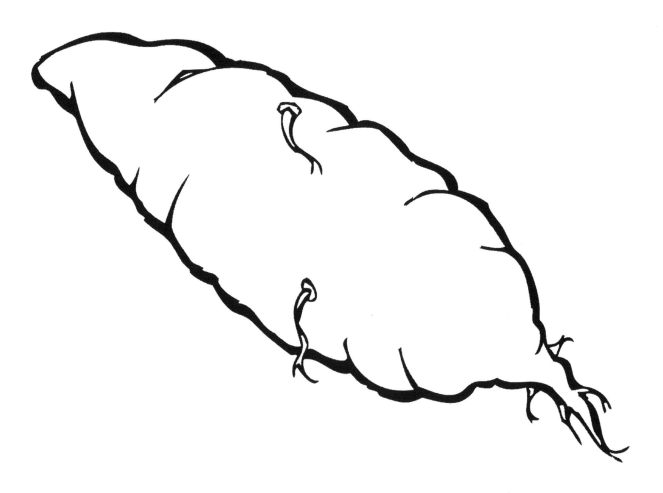

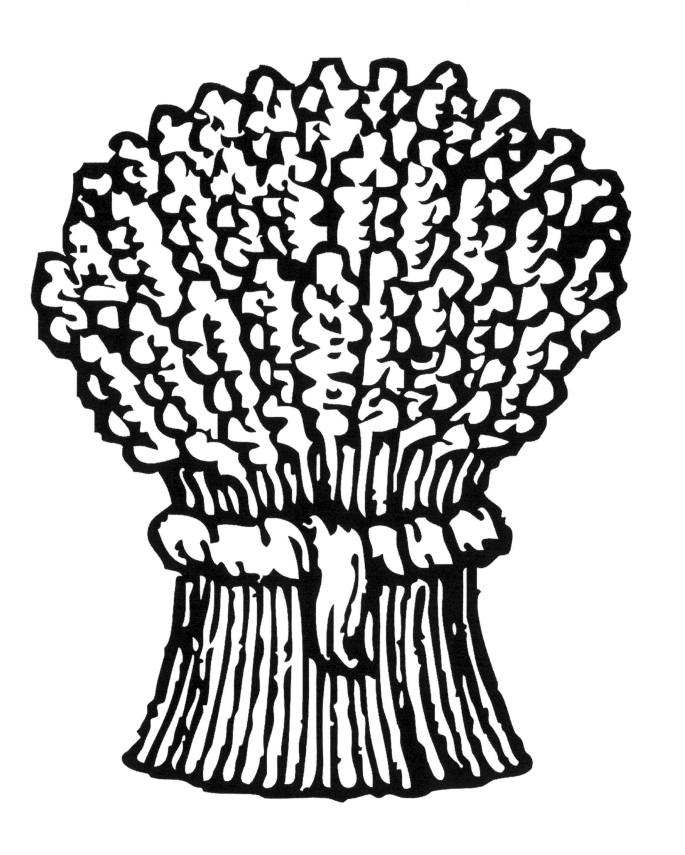

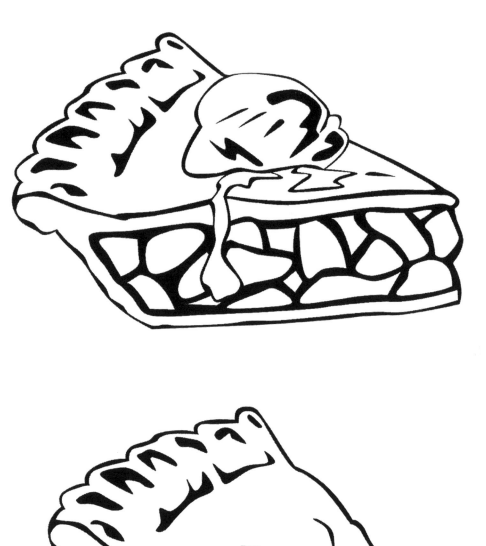
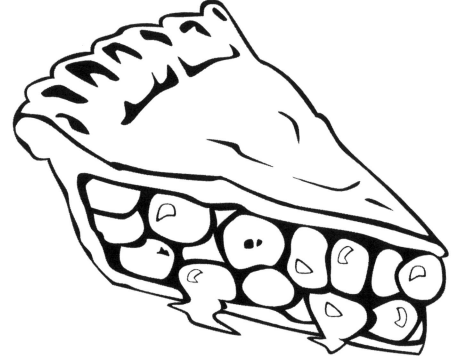

71062123R00037

Made in the USA
Lexington, KY
17 November 2017